The Journey
Receiving Our Endowment

JEREMY OAKES

The Journey – Receiving Our Endowment

JOURNEY TO THE FULLNESS
Seeking Further Light and Knowledge

Copyright © 2013 Jeremy Oakes

All rights reserved – Jeremy Oakes and Journeytothefullness.com

ISBN-10: 1491098511
ISBN-13: 978-1491098516

First Edition

For more information on this and other publications, please visit Journeytothefullness.com

Dedication

For all whom He has prepared to receive of the fullness.

"And it shall come to pass, that if you are faithful you shall receive the fulness of the record of John." (D&C 93:18)

The Journey – Receiving Our Endowment

Contents

	Author Forward	i
1	Let us "BECOME"	Pg 1
2	Become What?	Pg 3
3	Our Initiation – Course Syllabus	Pg 6
4	Washing / Justification	Pg 8
5	Anointing / Sanctification	Pg 13
6	Confirming-Sealing / Sanctification	Pg 15
7	Clothing / Purification	Pg 16
8	Before Class Starts	Pg 18
9	The Course – Lecture & Lab	Pg 21
10	Telestial Kingdom	Pg 32
11	Second Token	Pg 36
12	Terrestrial Kingdom	Pg 39
13	The "SURE" Sign	Pg 42
14	Course Final	Pg 45
	Afterward	Pg 46

THE JOURNEY – RECEIVING OUR ENDOWMENT

Author Forward

The endowment ceremony is a divinely inspired presentation in which individuals are shown in the temple, through many symbols, the path which leads to receiving one's true endowment. This true endowment is entrance into the celestial kingdom where our Father resides and to become Kings and Queens, Priests and Priestesses. The endowment ceremony outlines the journey each of us will take individually.

It is the intent of the author to present the initiatory and endowment ceremonies in a semi-transparent fashion to encourage individuals in their progression along the path, while being certain not to disclose specific signs, tokens, keywords or penalties that the author and other individuals have covenanted to never divulge – except at a certain place. This article will outline the distinct stages leading to exaltation and receiving that which our Father desires all to receive – our endowment.

The author recognizes that there are many layers of understanding and interpretation one can be taught through the endowment ceremony. It should be acknowledged by the reader that the author claims no authority on the matter other than individual inspiration through the spirit, revelation and personal experience. All readers are encouraged to gain their own understanding by those same means.

Jeremy Oakes

1 Let us "become"

A plan was set forth in the pre-existence that would allow us as individuals to progress and **become** as our Heavenly Parents. This plan is often referred to as "The Plan of Salvation" or "The Great Plan of Happiness". This plan outlines a journey that leads to eternal life and exaltation.

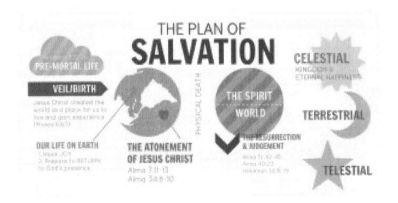

We will focus on these amazing gifts and do so with the perspective that they are available to us in this life - as there is

The Journey – Receiving Our Endowment

no specific mention of a physical death in the endowment ceremony.

> *"Line upon line, precept upon precept, here a little and there a little…".* (2 Nephi 28:30)

We will look at the different stages along the way to receiving our own endowment. As we do so, you are encouraged to remember the initiatory and the endowment ceremony that takes place in the temple. These ceremonies are heavenly inspired and divinely appointed to serve as a road map, full of powerful symbols and direction. Rely upon the spirit to teach you truth and to shine light into your soul. Seek, ponder, pray and participate in these sacred ceremonies. As you do, ask the Father through prayer "where am I on this journey".

Along this journey, if we continually press forward in obedience and faith in the Lord Jesus Christ, we will experience things that include, but are not limited to:

- Being "born again"
- Receiving the gift of the Holy Ghost
- Being washed – justified
- The ministering of angels
- Seeing visions
- Receiving revelation
- Hearing His voice
- Receiving our Calling & Election
- Being anointed – sanctified
- Feeling the prints in His hands

These will help us **"BECOME"**.

2 Become What?

We are children of heavenly parents - created in their image (Genesis 1:26-27, Moses 2:26-27, D&C 130:22). As their children we have great potential; we can become as they are. Just as a puppy grows to be an adult dog, and a baby grows to be an adult man, man can **become** as the Father and woman can **become** as the Mother.

> *"We are created, we are born for the express purpose of growing up from the low estate of manhood, to become Gods like unto our Father in heaven."* – Brigham Young (Journal of Discourses 3:93)

> *"As man now is, God once was: As God now is, man may be."* – Lorenzo Snow

While some individuals may consider it ignorant or disrespectful to believe we have the potential to become like our heavenly parents, our Savior Jesus Christ *"thought it not robbery to be equal with God…"* (Philippians 2:5-6).

The Journey – Receiving Our Endowment

In verse 7 of Philippians 2, we read that Jesus Christ *"...made himself of no reputation, and took upon him the form of a servant, and was made in the likeness of men..."* (Philippians 2:7). And yet, He would become like our Father.

To become like our Father the Savior did the work of the Father. The work of the Father is:

> *"...to bring to pass the immortality and eternal life of man."* (Moses 1:39)

Eternal life is the *"greatest gift of all the gifts of God"* (D&C 14:7), and it is given *"through Jesus Christ our Lord"* (Romans 6:23). Eternal life is to *"set down with [our] Father in his throne"* (Rev. 3:21), once we have overcome, have believed in Christ, and have *"...endure[d] to the end..."* (2 Nephi 33:4).

How much joy our heavenly parents must feel when a child of theirs grows closer to receiving eternal life!

> *"Remember the worth of souls is great in the sight of God..."* (D&C 18:10)

With this perspective - that we can receive eternal life and become as our heavenly parents, let's take a closer look at the path that has been laid before us in the works of the temple.

> *"Know ye not that ye are the temple of God, and that the Spirit of God dwelleth in you?"* (1 Corinthians 3:16)

In the temple we do work for the dead. This applies to us because we are as Adam – a fallen, natural man.

> *"...in the day that thou eatest thereof thou shalt surely die."* (Genesis 2:17)

We are temples. The temple is a symbol of us; we are not a symbol of the temple. We are meant to be holy and to house a god – as we are meant to become as He is. Currently we are fallen and dead. For the dead, temple work is required. The temple building shows us the work which is required to be done within us.

3 Our Initiation – Course Syllabus

A syllabus is an outline and summary of topics to be covered in a course. It should set clear expectations of what is to be presented and learned during the course. It provides a road map depicting the organization of the material, and it should be given at the start of the first session. Here is our syllabus – the Initiatory.

The initiatory is divided into four main parts. These parts consist of an individual being:

1. Washed
2. Anointed
3. Confirmed/Sealed
4. Clothed

During the initiatory - unlike most ordinances performed within the Church of Jesus Christ of Latter-day Saints, the officiator does not specify by what authority he or she acts. They merely state, "having authority". This is significant as it points to an issue of much concern and contention for many – both male and female; the issue being the understanding that only worthy *male* members can hold the priesthood. Regardless of one's understanding or view on the topic, it would seem that men and women hold the same authority to act in the ordinances of the initiatory. Keep in mind that this authority allows:

- Washing
- Anointing
- Confirming/Sealing
- Clothing

All of these processes are significant and separate ordinances that we can each participate in individually over the course of our journey. They are also contained in the endowment ceremony and this book will give an explanation of each ordinance. However, we are only reviewing the "syllabus" for now.

We should notice that during the initiatory ordinance, participants have each part of them washed. Each part of them is being anointed. Each part of them is being confirmed/sealed. This is significant and is a reflection of the all-encompassing power that each ordinance has on an individual once they occur.

As we consider these four stages, keep the following scripture in mind:

> *"For by the water ye keep the commandment; by the Spirit ye are **justified**, and by the blood ye are **sanctified**..."* (Moses 6:60, emphasis added.)

4 Washing / Justification

Keeping the commandments are a necessary part of the journey – but to an extent they do little other than to lead us to the spirit which justifies. We are not saved by the law or by keeping the law. The law serves to "cut us off" and act as a "schoolmaster".

> "And men are instructed sufficiently that they know good from evil. And the law is given unto men. And **by the law no flesh is justified**; or, **by the law men are cut off.** Yea, by the temporal law they were cut off; and also, by the spiritual law they perish from that which is good, and become miserable forever." (2 Nephi 2:5, emphasis added.)

> "Wherefore **the law was our schoolmaster** to bring us unto Christ, that we might be **justified by faith**." (Galatians 3:24, emphasis added.)

> "Knowing that a man is not justified by the works of the law, but by the faith of Jesus Christ, even we have believed in Jesus Christ, that we might **be justified by the faith of Christ**, and not

by the works of the law: for by the works of the law shall no flesh be justified." (Galatians 2:16, emphasis added.)

These scriptures teach us that:

- Men/women sufficiently know good from evil
- There are two parts to the law (temporal and spiritual)
- By the temporal law we are cut off and by the spiritual law we perish from that which is good
- The law is a schoolmaster that we might be justified
- Justification comes by faith and believing in Jesus Christ
- Justification does not come by works of the law

But what is justification? To be justified means to be free of blame and guilt. It is to be acquitted from sin and accepted. Those that believe are justified (Acts 13:39); we no longer *"perish from that which is good"* (2 Nephi 2:5). While the temporal law will not save us, meeting the qualifications of the spiritual law will justify us.

"Therefore we conclude that a man is justified by faith without the deeds of the law." (Romans 3:28)

"By the water ye keep the commandment; by the Spirit ye are justified..." (Moses 6:60).

By being baptized we keep the commandment, but it is by the spiritual baptism that we are justified. What does it take to experience this spiritual baptism?

"Wherefore, redemption cometh in and through the Holy Messiah; for he is full of grace and truth.

Behold, he offereth himself a sacrifice for sin, to answer the ends of the law, unto all those who have **a broken heart and a**

contrite spirit*; and unto none else can the ends of the law be answered."* (2 Nephi 2:6-7, emphasis added.)

It takes a broken heart and a contrite spirit. It does not take someone laying their hands on your head and stating, "receive the Holy Ghost". No, that declaration is a command and not a bestowal. With our baptism by water, we have kept the commandment. This is good and we will know based on the confirming feeling of the spirit.

Here is a great example of an individual having their sins forgiven and the guilt swept away:

> *"And I will tell you of the wrestle which I had before God, before I received a remission of my sins. Behold, I went to hunt beasts in the forests; and the words which I had often heard my father speak concerning eternal life, and the joy of the saints, sunk deep into my heart. And my soul hungered; and I kneeled down before my Maker, and I cried unto him in mighty prayer and supplication for mine own soul; and all the day long did I cry unto him; yea, and when the night came I did still raise my voice high that it reached the heavens. And there came a voice unto me, saying: Enos, thy sins are forgiven thee, and thou shalt be blessed. And I, Enos, knew that God could not lie;* **wherefore, my guilt was swept away.** *And I said: Lord, how is it done? And he said unto me:* **Because of thy faith in Christ...**" (Enos 1:2-8, emphasis added.)

This wasn't due to a fulfillment of the temporal law; this occurred because of a broken heart and contrite spirit.

This process of justification leads to receiving the Holy Ghost; a constant companion. We will come to see that this is the second token we receive in the endowment – the Holy Ghost. This event/process has many names, including but not limited to:

- Being "born again"
- The "mighty change"
- Baptism by fire
- Becoming clean
- Entering into the "strait and narrow path"
- Remission of sins

It is essential to experience this washing spiritually in order to enter the gate which leads to eternal life; there is no other way. Once you enter the gate, however, the work is not over.

> *"Wherefore, do the things which I have told you I have seen that your Lord and your Redeemer should do; for, for this cause have they been shown unto me, that ye might know the gate by which ye should enter.* **For the gate by which ye should enter is repentance and baptism by water; and then cometh a remission of your sins by fire and by the Holy Ghost.** *And then are ye in this strait and narrow path which leads to eternal life; yea, ye have entered in by the gate; ye have done according to the commandments of the Father and the Son; and ye have received the Holy Ghost, which witnesses of the Father and the Son, unto the fulfilling of the promise which he hath made, that if ye entered in by the way ye should receive. And now, my beloved brethren, after ye have gotten into this strait and narrow path,* **I would ask if all is done? Behold, I say unto you, Nay;** *for ye have not come thus far save it were by the word of Christ with unshaken faith in him, relying wholly upon the merits of him who is mighty to save."* (2 Nephi 31:17-19, emphasis added.)

Before we allow ourselves to dismiss the importance of baptism by water, we should notice that it is mentioned in the previous scripture. Also, we will find it is mentioned in the endowment ceremony. It is the change that occurs when we symbolically take our shoes off.

The Journey – Receiving Our Endowment

Once the justification has been completed, you enter the sanctification stage.

5 Anointing / Sanctification

To sanctify is to: make holy; set apart as sacred; consecrate.

In this stage we are making our ghost *holy*. We have received the Holy Ghost as our constant companion and we are continuing along the path to eternal life. During this process we will have HIS spirit to always be with us.

Let's look at the end of the sacramental prayers; they are similar enough to illustrate this point so we will just use one as an example:

> "*...take upon them the name of thy* **Son**, *and always remember* **him**, *and keep* **his** *commandments which* **he** *hath given them, that they may always have* **his Spirit** *to be with them. Amen.*" (Moroni 4:3, emphasis added.)

As many are aware, the sacrament is intended to be taken by those who have been baptized. If we focus on the words of the sacrament prayer, we will notice two things: first, that we are not "renewing" a covenant, we are taking upon us the name of the Son and being willing to keep his commandments. Second, we are doing this so that we can always have HIS spirit to be with us.

In the justification stage we experienced the baptism by fire; the mighty change; being born again. By experiencing this, we gained the constant companionship of the Holy Ghost.

Remember that *"by the Spirit ye are justified"* (Moses 6:60). By receiving this change, we have been justified and this has brought us through a gate that enables us to have another companion along the path – Jesus Christ.

Remember that *"by the blood ye are sanctified"* (Moses 6:60). In this stage we are being sanctified by Christ. Much like the Old Testament teaches the letter of the law, and the New Testament teaches the spirit of the law, the justification stage was largely based on the letter of the law - while the sanctification stage is based on the spirit of the law. Where we were once taught, *"thou shalt not commit adultery"* (Exodus 20:14), we are now in the stage where we understand, *"...whosoever looketh on a woman to lust after her hath committed adultery with her already in his heart"* (Matthew 5:28).

Notice who gives this law; Jesus Christ. Notice whose spirit we are to always have with us after justification; Jesus Christ. The law comes from Him - as He is always with us. He is leading and guiding us along the path of sanctification. We entered the gate and now we are progressing along the path.

6 Confirming-Sealing / Sanctification

In this stage, we are closing or sealing the sanctification stage. We have progressed to a point where we are holy and we are confirmed. Notice here though, that in the initiatory it is not done by the same individual who anointed you. This is noteworthy and should be considered.

7 Clothing / Purification

> *"For by the water ye keep the commandment; by the Spirit* ye are **justified**, *and by the blood ye are* **sanctified**..." (Moses 6:60, emphasis added.)

What about the perfection part? By the Father we are made perfect. Recall in the New Testament where Jesus said:

> *"Be ye therefore perfect, even as your Father which is in heaven is perfect."* (Matthew 5:48)

A similar statement is made in the Book of Mormon when Jesus said:

> *"Therefore I would that ye should be perfect even as I, or your Father who is in heaven is perfect."* (3 Nephi 12:48)

What is the difference? In the New Testament or pre-death, Jesus doesn't refer to Himself as being perfect. But in the Book of Mormon or post-death, He does refer to Himself as being perfect. What changed? The resurrection is the difference; not just the resurrection, but going to the Father.

> *"Jesus saith unto her, Hold me not; for I am not yet ascended to my Father: but go to my brethren, and say unto them, I ascend unto my Father, and your Father; and to my God, and your God."* (John 20:17)

Throughout this book, we will see that the kingdoms of glory each have different laws, and each kingdom serves the purpose of a specific process. At the same time, we will see that each kingdom has an officiator to bring about the work relative to that kingdom. It just so happens, that the celestial kingdom is the place the Father does His work - and that is to clothe.

> *"I will greatly rejoice in the Lord, my soul shall be joyful in my God; for he hath clothed me with the garments of salvation, he hath covered me with the robe of righteousness, as a bridegroom decketh himself with ornaments, and as a bride adorneth herself with her jewels."* (Isaiah 61:10)

The word "clothed" here in the Greek language, is "enduo", which is the root for our English word "endow". The initiatory is an initiation into the process of being clothed or endowed, and the process of being endowed is to be clothed in the robes of the holy priesthood.

This is the work of the Father. These are different than the garments of the holy priesthood as they are temporary "until you have finished your work on the earth". While the garments are temporary, the robes are such that they will not be removed.

8 Before Class Starts

This might be an appropriate time to draw a few parallels between the initiatory and the endowment before class starts. We will cover these in more detail later, but for the sake of understanding the initiatory, we will briefly introduce the four tokens and what they represent.

These four tokens are:

1. The First Token of the Aaronic Priesthood
2. The Second Token of the Aaronic Priesthood
3. The First Token of the Melchizedek Priesthood
4. The Second Token of the Melchizedek Priesthood

In order, we may refer to them through this article as:

1. The First Token
2. The Second Token
3. The Third Token
4. The Fourth Token

These tokens represent:

1. The light of Christ
2. The Holy Ghost
3. Receiving our Calling and Election and the companionship of HIS spirit
4. The Second Comforter

The part of the endowment when each of these tokens are given is significant; the sphere/light/room/kingdom they are given within, is significant. Remember that this ceremony is one that happens in this life. Each one of these tokens has a name which we will not divulge in this book. Please remember them and be mindful of when the last name is given. Also, each token has a sign that accompanies it. We will not divulge these signs either, but please remember them and be mindful that the signs are given after the tokens.

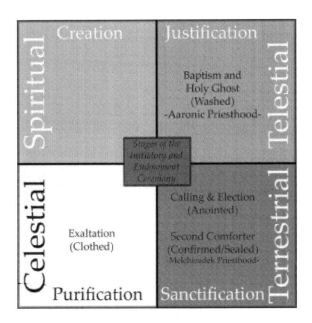

The Journey – Receiving Our Endowment

These tokens, names, and signs do have a place in the initiatory. The initiatory has four "rooms", and each room represents a portion of the endowment:

1. Creation
2. Justification
3. Sanctification
4. Purification

Each of these is represented in the endowment as a "room":

1. Garden
2. Telestial
3. Terrestrial
4. Celestial

And each room serves a specific purpose:

1. Created
2. Washed
3. Anointed and confirmed
4. Clothed

Remember these as we delve into the endowment ceremony.

9 THE COURSE – LECTURE & LAB

At a point early in the endowment ceremony, we are told of three persons and who they represent: Elohim, Jehovah, and Michael. According to Elohim's command, Jehovah and Michael go down and organize a world. They also organize man in their own image; male and female.

There comes a time during the presentation that we are told we must consider ourselves as if we were respectively, Adam and Eve. At first it may seem as if this presentation is merely a history lesson. Then our understanding increases, and we begin to recognize our roles as men and women. But there is another level of understanding after that (and there is probably another after that as well.) For now we are going to examine this presentation – not as a history, or as an aid to better understand our roles as men and women, but rather we are going to approach this as if this lesson pertains to you, and YOU.

All things were created spiritually before they were created physically or temporally (Moses 3:5,7). Adam was created before Eve and it was by a rib which the Lord God had taken from the man (Moses 3:21-22). Then Adam says:

> *"This I know now is bone of my bones, and flesh of my flesh...she was taken out of man"* (Moses 3:23).

Remember that the creation story we have is one given to Moses – who in turn was trying to share and teach the children of Israel. History shows that these children were slow to learn and were given a strict law of carnal commandments, along with the preparatory gospel. The creation story is very symbolic and elementary - as it was originally given to a people who hardened their hearts and could not endure God's presence (D&C 84:24-27).

Due to the symbolic and elementary nature of the creation presentation, we often do not know what to take literally and what to take figuratively. What we know is that we are supposed to consider ourselves as Adam and Eve, respectively. But how respectively? We are going to approach this as if each of us individually - are both Adam and Eve. Adam was created first; Adam will represent the spirit. Eve was created second; she will represent the physical/natural man. So we will consider ourselves as if we are spirit and body, respectively.

It is interesting to note that our physical/natural body appears as our spirit body (Ether 3:16). In this sense, Eve was created in the image of Adam. She was created from one of Adam's ribs. They took a part of Adam (an image), and made Eve. Or in other words, our physical/natural body was created in the image of our spirit body.

In making this connection - that Adam represents the spirit and Eve represents the body, it should be noted that it is not the intent of this book to suggest that the female is intended to be subservient to the male in any form. Even though the endowment presentation conveys many images that could be interpreted to suggest that, this book does not subscribe to that line of thought. Men and women are treated in this article as equals. They are both allowed to – and have the opportunity to receive of the fullness. A woman should read this article as if Adam is her spirit, and Eve is her body – just as a man should do the same.

Adam is given Eve (Moses 3:23), and told:

> *"...here is a woman whom we have formed and whom we give unto you to be a companion and helpmeet for you".*

Did not our Father form this body of ours? Is not our body **intended** to be a companion and helpmeet for us?

> *"For man is spirit. The elements are eternal, and spirit and element, inseparably connected, receive a fulness of joy; And when separated, man cannot receive a fulness of joy."* (D&C 93:33-34)

Regardless, our body does get us into trouble. Remember, our body is physical/natural. Natural implies *the natural man* – which is an enemy to God, and has been from the fall of Adam... but not *before* the fall (Mosiah 3:19).

Adam and Eve are introduced into the garden and commanded to multiply and replenish the earth – that they may have joy and rejoicing in their posterity. They are also given to eat freely of every tree in the garden except from the tree of knowledge of good and evil. Nevertheless, they may choose for themselves, for they are given their agency. But in the day they eat, they shalt surely die.

After these instructions are given, we are told that Elohim and Jehovah withdraw from the garden but that they shall visit again and give further instructions.

The Journey – Receiving Our Endowment

The next event is the approach of Lucifer. He informs Adam of a new world; apparently Adam knows nothing about any other world. Lucifer comments that his eyes have not yet been opened and that Adam has forgotten everything. At this point Lucifer tries to persuade Adam (who is our spirit) to partake of the forbidden fruit. He tells Adam it will make him wise. Adam (our spirit) is valiant and remembers the command of his Father. Lucifer tries yet again to persuade Adam by telling him that he will not surely die, but he shall be as the gods – knowing good and evil (Moses 4:11).

The spirit holds out well, and Lucifer (our opposition) decides to focus his sights on Eve (our body). Temptation walks right up to our body and offers the forbidden fruit along with a promise: *"It will make you wise"*. Here, Eve (our natural man) does something interesting that our spirit did not do. Eve asks: *"who are you"*? This suggests a few things: Adam might have recognized the opposition, but the natural man/body is not able to discern on its own. It might also suggest that our spirit doesn't care who or what the opposition is, it desires to do the will of the Father. Either way, Eve partakes of the fruit.

Conventional wisdom within The Church of Jesus Christ of Latter-day Saints suggests that Eve was making a wise choice (Moses 5:11). From a historical perspective, this may be true (Eve *was* seen in vision amongst the noble spirits as noted in D&C 138:39). However, we are looking at this from an individual perspective - as it pertains to us as spirits and bodies. From this viewpoint, we see how our natural man is more subject to the enticing of the opposition, and often used to lure the spirit into spiritual death.

Once Eve offers Adam the fruit – which she now describes as *"delicious to the taste and very desirable"*, Adam is faced with a scenario in which he is about to be separated from Eve and left alone – unable to fulfill the other commands. Adam recognizes the situation and chooses to partake – *"that man may be"*.

This seems to make Lucifer happy. Interestingly enough, Eve **now** recognizes Lucifer as *"he who was cast out of Father's presence for rebellion"*, and Adam wants to know *"what is that apron you have on"*. The opposition is about to come very close to both the spirit and body – and on a constant basis, except for a few occasions and until they progress into a greater degree of light.

Adam and Eve - with the command from Lucifer: *"See, you are naked. Take some fig leaves..."* recognize that they are naked. They quickly hide – out of fear that the Father will see them.

At this point in the endowment ceremony, we put on an apron. This apron will serve as a symbol to remind us of our agency. We could focus on what the fig leaves attempted to cover; Adam and Eve's transgression. However, clearly it was not a sufficient covering for the transgression. We will focus on the apron/fig leaves as being a reminder of our agency and our knowledge of good and evil. This will be explained further when Adam and Eve are clothed and expelled from the garden.

When Elohim returns, He has to call for Adam three times. This may be suggestive of the three kingdoms. If we think of these kingdoms as a state of being rather than physical locations, it will bring clarity to the fact that Elohim resides in the highest kingdom (the celestial). He calls for Adam there, but Adam doesn't answer. Elohim moves to the kingdom beneath it (the terrestrial). He calls again, but Adam does not respond. Finally, He moves to the furthest kingdom (the telestial). He calls for Adam again and this time Adam reveals himself.

The Journey – Receiving Our Endowment

"*I heard thy voice and hid myself, because I was naked*", is Adam's reply. Adam is asked a few questions and he retorts that it was the woman that was given to him – that he should remain with, who gave him the fruit, and he did eat. This might seem as a cop-out or a lame excuse by Adam, but spiritually, we should be able to relate. Isn't it interesting how our natural man/body has desires that often overpower our spiritual desires? Don't we spiritually recognize our guilt – but also recognize that it was our body and the desires of the natural man that caught us?

Eve recognizes that it was the opposition who beguiled and enticed her: "*The serpent beguiled me, and I did eat*". Our bodies are tricked; we are offered promises with those temptations that provide immediate gratification. The promise might include knowledge, wisdom, or joy and happiness. Every time however, we succumb to a lie whose fruit is not delicious and not desirable – though our body might first recognize it as such.

In the exchange that follows, Lucifer is expelled from the garden. However, before being commanded to depart, he manages to give this message:

> "*...I will take the spirits that follow me, and they shall possess the bodies thou createst for Adam and Eve!*
>
> *...I will take the treasures of the earth, and with gold and silver I will buy up armies and navies, false priests who oppress and tyrants who destroy and reign with blood and horror on the earth!*" (LDS Temple Endowment)

We can learn many things from these few statements, but the basic lesson might come down to the following: Lucifer is not alone. He has those who follow him and do his work. He is against us and he will use the things of the world to oppress and destroy us.

Now we approach the conditions of the fall. Cherubim and a flaming sword are placed to guard the way of the tree of life - lest Adam put forth his hand and partake of the fruit and live forever in his sins (Moses 4:31, Alma 42:2). Why was this done?

> *"And now behold, I say unto you that if it had been possible for Adam to have partaken of the fruit of the tree of life at that time, there* **would have been no death***, and the word would have been void,* **making God a liar***, for he said: If thou eat thou shalt surely die."* (Alma 12:23, emphasis added.)

> *"And thus we see, that there was a time granted unto man to repent, yea, a probationary time, a time to repent and serve God. For behold, if Adam had put forth his hand immediately, and partaken of the tree of life,* **he would have lived forever***, according to the word of God, having no space for repentance; yea, and also the word of God would have been void, and the great plan of salvation would have been frustrated. But behold, it was appointed unto man to die—therefore, as they were cut off from the tree of life they should be cut off from the face of the earth—and man became lost forever, yea, they became fallen man. And now, ye see by this that our first parents were cut off both temporally and spiritually from the presence of the Lord; and thus we see they became subjects to follow after their own will."* (Alma 42:4-7, emphasis added.)

Before being cut off from His presence however, Eve makes a covenant to obey the law of the Lord and to hearken to Adam's counsel – as he hearkens to the Father. This covenant will be of particular significance later. If Eve is the natural man/body, and Adam is the spirit, at what point has the spirit hearkened and obeyed the counsel and command of the Father? One would think that if the spirit had indeed obeyed the Father, then the body would have to fulfill its covenant and obey the counsel of the spirit.

This might cause one to be curious; why are bodies sick, frail, wounded, broken, etc.? This will be addressed later as we look at the true order of prayer and notice the natural man/body veiling its face, while the spirit unites with the sealing grip – placing an arm of authority on the body's shoulder. For now though, it is sufficient to note that the natural man/body is intended to be a helpmeet to the spirit. It is intended that our bodies hearken to the desires of our spirit. Whether or not this relationship actually occurs is a different matter.

Adam makes a covenant with Elohim:

> *"I now covenant with thee that from this time forth I will obey thy law and keep thy commandments."* (LDS Temple Endowment)

It is noteworthy, that at this point, Elohim acknowledges Adam's (the spirit's) covenant, but no specific acknowledgement is made towards Eve's (natural man/body's) covenant with Adam. This is because Elohim recognizes the covenants we make spiritually. Physical covenants are only symbols representing those covenants that are spiritual. Elohim is less concerned with the obedience of our bodies to Him, and more concerned with our spirit's obedience. Remember, our body is a helpmeet for our spirit. Our body is meant to hearken to our spirit; our spirit hearkens to Elohim.

At this point, Elohim instructs Jehovah to make coats of skin to cover Adam and Eve's nakedness (Moses 4:27). You will remember that the apron can be seen to represent our transgression – in which case, the fig leaves are not sufficient to cover our transgression. However, the coats of skin are sufficient to cover our nakedness. *"Coats of skin"* implies that an animal was sacrificed on our behalf to cover our nakedness – just as the Lamb of God was sacrificed to provide sufficient means to cover our nakedness. However, after being clothed in the garments of the holy priesthood, we still wear this apron on top of our other clothing. This is why it is a symbol reminding us of our agency, not necessarily our transgression or sin. It is our agency and knowledge of good and evil that chooses to progress along this path. At each stage in the endowment, this fig leaf is on top. We always have the choice to take upon ourselves these sacred covenants – or reject them. We wear our aprons into the celestial kingdom; into the Father's presence, where no unclean thing can enter.

> *"And no unclean thing can enter into his kingdom; therefore nothing entereth into his rest save it be those who have washed their garments in my blood, because of their faith, and the repentance of all their sins, and their faithfulness unto the end."* (3 Nephi 27:19)

Again, our aprons are not a symbol of our sins, they are a symbol of our agency, and the knowledge of good and evil. At this stage of the endowment each individual makes a covenant and enters into the "law of obedience". The sisters (natural man/body) covenant before God, angels and the other witnesses, that they will hearken to their husband's (spirit) counsel – as he hearkens to the Father. The brethren (spirit) covenant before the same witnesses, that they will obey the law of God and keep His commandments.

Once we have covenanted to be obedient, we are given the "law of sacrifice".

> *"…and they heard the voice of the Lord from the way toward the Garden of Eden, speaking unto them, and they saw him not; for they were shut out from his presence. And he gave unto them commandments, that they should worship the Lord their God, and should offer the firstlings of their flocks, for an offering unto the*

Lord. And Adam was obedient unto the commandments of the Lord." (Moses 5:4-5)

The laws of obedience and sacrifice are accompanied by the first token of the Aaronic Priesthood. This token comes with a name and a sign. We are given this token before Adam and Eve are expelled from the garden. This is an indication of when we as individuals receive this token, and what the token is. Every person receives something before they come into this mortal existence:

> *"And that I am the true light that lighteth every man that cometh into the world."* (D&C 93:2)

This token is "the light of Christ":

> *"For behold, the Spirit of Christ is given to every man, that he may know good from evil; wherefore, I show unto you the way to judge; for every thing which inviteth to do good, and to persuade to believe in Christ, is sent forth by the power and gift of Christ; wherefore ye may know with a perfect knowledge it is of God.*
>
> *But whatsoever thing persuadeth men to do evil, and believe not in Christ, and deny him, and serve not God, then ye may know with a perfect knowledge it is of the devil; for after this manner doth the devil work, for he persuadeth no man to do good, no, not one; neither do his angels; neither do they who subject themselves unto him."* (Moroni 7:16-17)

The scripture above mentions two entities who persuade an individual to do good, or to do evil. These "voices" we hear are either of God, or of the devil. It makes sense that there would be a third "voice" we would hear; that "voice" is YOU. There is a conversation in which the light of Christ directs you to do something good – followed by the voice of the opposition persuading you not to do that thing which is good.

The conversation might look something like this:

- *Light of Christ says* – Make the bed.
- *Opposition says* – Making the bed will take time and the blankets are just going to get messed up in a few hours anyway... and you have other things you can do... and your back hurts... and...
- YOU say – Hmmm... should I make the bed? It is going to get messed up in a few hours. I do have other things I could be doing that are fun. My back does hurt...

Notice how "the YOU voice" is the one being persuaded, while the other voices are giving direction and suggestion. Also, notice that the direction or command is good – while the suggestions coming from the opposition are appeasing to the desires of the flesh and the natural man. In order to progress correctly in this scenario, it requires obedience and sacrifice – for which one will be rewarded. When we are continually obedient to the light of Christ, we are progressing along the path to eternal life and coming unto the Father (D&C 84:47).

At this point in the endowment presentation, Adam and Eve have been expelled from the garden into the lone and dreary world – where they may learn from their own experience to distinguish good from evil. So far, Adam and Eve have only received the law of obedience and the law of sacrifice. We now enter into mortality and the telestial kingdom.

10 TELESTIAL KINGDOM

Adam builds an altar and begins to pray. He utters a phrase three times – which is significant and might relate to the three kingdoms, as well as the understanding we have that Elohim called for Adam 3 times. Adam is looking for messengers from his Father, but for the time, he has an audience with Lucifer – wherein Adam and Lucifer share a short exchange. At no point does Eve participate in the discussion other than to be present. This is not to suggest that we experience the same, this is teaching us how we should interact with the opposition. Our spirit should lead the body. All too often in our lives we experience the opposite – the body leading the spirit.

Elohim sends messengers to visit Adam (with no mention of Eve) in the telestial world – and without disclosing their identity. Elohim wants these messengers to observe the conditions there and see if Adam (again, no mention of Eve) has been true to the token and sign given him in the garden.

Remember that the first token is the light of Christ. Being true to this token would suggest being true to the laws of obedience and sacrifice. The messengers would ultimately find that Adam was true to this token.

Moses expounds upon this:

> "...*they heard the voice of the Lord from the way toward the Garden of Eden, speaking unto them,* **and they saw him not***; for they were shut out from his presence.*
>
> **And he gave unto them commandments**, *that they should worship the Lord their God, and should offer the firstlings of their flocks...*" (Moses 5:4-5, emphasis added.)

How did they receive the commandment when *"they saw him not"*? It was by the light of Christ – the source that persuades mankind to do good. The light of Christ is the source of commandments. So, Adam heard the command, or in other words, the light of Christ was a token he still had. But was he obedient?

> *"And after many days an angel of the Lord appeared unto Adam, saying: Why dost thou offer sacrifices unto the Lord? And Adam said unto him: I know not, save the Lord commanded me."* (Moses 5:6)

Yes, he was obedient and he did sacrifice. The messengers found that Adam was true and faithful to the token and sign given to him in the garden. Adam was not willing to sell them for money – though he had them. In other words, our spirit should not be willing to be persuaded by the things of this world that would have us disobey God.

At this stage of the ceremony, the messenger commends Adam for his integrity, and lets him know that he shall probably be visited again.

If we look back at Moses 5:6, it says, *"I know not, save the Lord commanded me"*. Often we receive direction from the light of Christ and know not why. The important thing here is obedience. This is important because once we have been found true to the token given to us – meaning, once we have been obedient and have sacrificed according to the light of Christ, we put ourselves in a position to receive another visit – and ultimately the second token.

> **"And in that day the Holy Ghost fell upon Adam**, *which beareth record of the Father and the Son, saying: I am the Only Begotten of the Father from the beginning, henceforth and forever, that as thou hast fallen thou mayest be redeemed, and all mankind, even as many as will."* (Moses 5:9, emphasis added.)

"And in that day the Holy Ghost fell upon Adam…" – We will next look at the second token of the Aaronic Priesthood; the Holy Ghost. But, before we do, let's look at a real-life example pertaining to how this first token works and leads us to receiving the second token.

Two missionaries (representing true messengers) knock on the door of a busy home. An individual answers the door and the missionaries proceed to offer the sharing of a message about Jesus Christ and His gospel. The individual immediately hears the three voices:

- *Light of Christ says* – Let them in.

- *Opposition says* – Letting them in will take time and the house is a mess… and they are Mormons!… and the kids are going nuts… and the dog is barking… and they are Mormons!… and dinner is cooking… and they are Mormons!… and…

- *YOU say* – Hmmm… should I let them in? The house is a mess. They are Mormons – weird… the kids are jumping off the counter with an umbrella… they are Mormons – weird… I don't know about them… I should finish cooking dinner… or start… but I can tell them I am currently cooking dinner……. Oh FINE… Come on in.

At this point a number of things have happened; but for the sake of this topic, the illustration shows that the individual listened to the light of Christ. If things progress and they take the challenge to read the Book of Mormon (obedience and sacrifice), and sincerely asking through prayer if it is His word… then something happens: the Holy Ghost bears witness of the truth. The individual has not yet received the gift or constant companionship of the Holy Ghost, but they received comfort (the first comforter), and a witness that the book is true and confirmation that the messengers are of God.

11 Second Token

In the ceremony, before Adam is given a new law (the law of the Gospel), there is an exchange of the first token. Because this exchange occurs, Adam proclaims: *"Now I know that you are true messengers sent down from Father"*. The token isn't what brought about this knowledge; it was the influence of the Holy Ghost.

We then come to the reception of the law of the gospel; the preparatory gospel of *"repentance and of baptism, and the remission of sins, and the law of carnal commandments"* (D&C 84:27). We first put our robes on the left shoulder. This is symbolic of the physical baptism by water – and though this does cause a change, it is not the change necessary to entering the terrestrial law. Remember that we are not saved by the law; by the water we keep the commandments but it is by the spirit that we are justified (Moses 6:60). At this point, we take our shoes off; that's what we do when we are baptized by water. Notice later, however, that when we change our robes to the right shoulder - we leave our shoes on. Baptism by fire doesn't happen in a font. It might happen at work, in the car, on the couch, on a mountain, etc. The point is that your shoes might be on.

After putting the robes on the left shoulder (being baptized by water) and receiving the second token, a process is started called "justification". We are now being washed by the spirit. At this stage in our lives we feel the influence of the Holy Ghost, and it truly is a gift. However, we have not yet experienced "the mighty change" that will cause the Holy Ghost to be our constant companion. This process of justification has just begun.

The messengers return and report. They are then instructed to return to Adam and clothe him in the robes of the holy priesthood, with the robe on the right shoulder. This is to prepare him to officiate in the ordinances of the Melchizedek Priesthood. The Aaronic Priesthood is a symbol of the Melchizedek Priesthood; where one is physical, the other is spiritual; where one is left, the other is right. When we experience being "born again", it is a "mighty change". It's as if we are changing our robes from the left shoulder to the right. Once this process has occurred we are prepared to officiate in the ordinances of the Melchizedek Priesthood and be brought into a new kingdom or sphere – with a new law.

The next portion of the endowment requires action on our part – just as the other portions required action. We need to get up and move to the next room. We need to accept that we have received the second token, and recognize that a new sphere is available to us. This is vital because without doing so, we limit our progression and the opportunity to receive the third token.

Some individuals may find themselves stuck at this point. Sometimes it is because they don't know where to go.. Sometimes it is because they have not *accepted* the gift offered. Sometimes it is both. This stage was representative of the stage of justification- which is completed by the spirit and not by our works. Too often we feel as if perfection is required; this is not the case. We need to qualify – which is different than earning. We cannot earn our salvation. If we were capable of earning salvation, there would be no need for a Savior; the debt is paid once we qualify. We only offer a small portion of the payment but it is all we are capable of offering. Our payment is a broken heart and a contrite spirit (2 Nephi 2:7). We are broken because we know there is no hope of us solving the problem. We are broken to pay the debt. We are contrite because we are submissive and humble. We acknowledge that we need relief. We see that without Him, we cannot enter the gate.

Surprisingly, the debt can be paid. We need to simply have faith in Christ and believe that our sins can be forgiven. We need to believe that the power of the atonement can even remove the unrighteous desires of our hearts; not simply help us suppress them, but to fully and completely remove them.

"...their hearts had been changed; that they had no more desire to do evil." (Alma 19:33)

If we do not believe our very nature can be changed, then we do not have faith in the atonement; we do not believe in Jesus Christ as our Savior. And if we do not believe in Him, we are not able to enter the gate.

The good news is that individuals can have their very natures changed. They can be born again. They can – and do experience the "mighty change". This is as real and tangible as changing your robes to the other shoulder. You can feel the blood in your veins boiling – on fire from head to toe. The baptism by fire is real and it is a result of faith in Jesus Christ.

12 Terrestrial Kingdom

Upon entering into the terrestrial kingdom, we should notice a few things:

- We no longer hear from Satan – we no longer have to entertain his words
- The light is brighter
- We no longer change our robes
- All tokens are related to Christ

The first law we are given is the law of chastity. This might be confusing to those who seek to understand the endowment ceremony. One might ask themselves, "isn't the law of chastity part of the law of the gospel?" The answer is, yes. But in this kingdom, we are progressing to a higher law. Just as the Old Testament taught a lower law than the New Testament, the telestial kingdom has a lower law than the terrestrial kingdom. Just as we were once taught *"thou shalt not commit adultery"* (Exodus 20:14), we are now taught, *"...that whosoever looketh on a woman to lust after her hath committed adultery with her already in his heart"* (Matthew 5:28). This is a new law. This is a higher law.

Nephi experienced this paradigm shift when he was commanded to kill Laban. Nephi knew the law of Moses. According to that law you are not to kill. Nephi was well aware and he "shrunk" (1 Nephi 4:10) that he might not slay Laban. But the spirit gave command again. Three times, Nephi received the command and then the reason was revealed:

> *"Behold the Lord slayeth the wicked to bring forth his righteous purposes. It is better that one man should perish than that a nation should dwindle and perish in unbelief."* (1 Nephi 4:13)

The law did not change; Nephi changed. Nephi was entering into the terrestrial kingdom. *"Thou shalt not kill"* was a telestial law. In the terrestrial sphere, the law (under the direction of the spirit) said: *"It is better that one man should perish than that a nation should dwindle and perish in unbelief"* (1 Nephi 4:13).

This is what is being taught at this stage of the endowment. We have been justified, and now we are being sanctified. We have fulfilled the law in us to be justified. Now we are concerned with the spirit of the law – not the letter of the law. We are no longer bound by the letter because that was the law of the telestial; we are not bound by that kingdom. We are bound by the spirit – and this law might be in direct contradiction to the lesser law. No need to fear, our exaltation is not dependent upon the telestial law. Our exaltation is dependent upon keeping His commandments – even if they contradict the established understanding of the gospel law.

> *"And now, when I, Nephi, had heard these words, I remembered the words of the Lord which he spake unto me in the wilderness, saying that: Inasmuch as thy seed shall keep my commandments, they shall prosper in the land of promise."* (1 Nephi 4:14)

Upon receiving this law we receive the third token. This token is a "sign", and the name associated with it is significant. This token is symbolic of receiving your calling and election – the gift of eternal life and exaltation.

> *"I would exhort you to go on and continue to call upon God until you make your calling and election sure for yourselves, by obtaining this more sure word of prophecy, and wait patiently for the promise until you obtain it."* (Teachings of the Prophet Joseph Smith, p. 299)

Calling and election is a promise, and this promise has a name and sign associated with it. Again, the name of this token is significant. It is referred to as a "sign". However, it is not the "sure sign".

Upon receiving your calling and election, further light and knowledge is poured out to you in a way you have never experienced before. A flood of truth enters your soul and you know what it is like to have the constant companionship of the Holy Ghost.

In this kingdom and law, you also have another constant companion. Remember back to the earlier words regarding the sacrament. We are now in the stage of being sanctified. We have been baptized and now we partake of the sacrament. In doing this – so we might always have HIS spirit to be with us. Again, the work of this kingdom is the work of Jesus Christ. Here, at this stage of receiving the third token, we will experience visions and dreams in which we can see Him, hear Him, and feel Him. This is in the spirit and thus it serves as a "sign". A sign of whom? The Son.

In this stage we are learning new laws and being sanctified by Christ. *"By the blood ye are sanctified…"* (Moses 6:60). The process is not complete though – we still need to receive the fourth token.

13 THE "SURE" SIGN

This token is a "sure sign". We will not receive the name of this token until it is time to progress to the next law or kingdom. This token is symbolic of receiving the Second Comforter; it truly is a "sure sign". You know both physically and spiritually that Jesus is the Christ. You know spiritually because you have been in His presence through vision and dream. You now know physically because your body has touched His body. You have been sealed to Him. The token is exchanged in a grip that is symbolic of sealing.

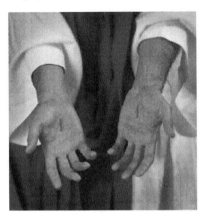

This is because you truly are sealed to Him. You have become one with Him and you are shortly going to be presented to the Father – that you might be one with Him as well. All that you have is now His. This is the law of consecration. However, it is misunderstood at times. While all that you have is His, all that He has is about to be yours as well.

Before being presented to the Father, an invitation will be extended. Those who wish to participate will be taught "the true order of prayer". This prayer is symbolic of a work to be done. Not all will participate; it is not required of you to participate in order to progress. During this work, all the signs and names will be expressed. The tokens will not be shared though. You do not receive anything but the joy of serving. In this "prayer", Eve will veil her face and Adam will take hold of her by a sealing grip. A work will commence, and once that work is complete, the "seal" will be broken.

Again, this is a work that is voluntary. It is a symbol of translation and the purpose of such an ordinance. At translation, the body is commanded to hearken to the council of the spirit. This is why Eve veils her face. At this point the body now has to hearken to the desires of the spirit – because now the spirit has hearkened to Elohim.

> *"I now covenant with thee that from this time forth I will obey thy law and keep thy commandments."* (LDS Temple Endowment)

All through the telestial law and kingdom we are living the preparatory gospel. This gospel is not complete and until one has received the fullness, one cannot keep His commandments. Thus, in the telestial sphere, our bodies do not have to hearken to the counsel of our spirits.

The Journey – Receiving Our Endowment

The body and spirit are sealed together for a time; this is why the sealing grip is used. Once the work is complete, there is a separation or a change before receiving the name of the forth token. (See: 3 Nephi 28.)

14 Course Final

The wrap up scene of the endowment commences when an individual receives the name of the forth token. This name has two key parts. One part is physical in nature, and the other is spiritual. They are given together – to be together for time and all eternity. Brothers and sisters, this is receiving your endowment; being clothed in the robes of the holy priesthood, to never have them removed. Perfection is not required. That stage is the work of the Father in His kingdom. We must have faith in Jesus Christ. He truly is the gate.

Afterward

The purpose of this book is to cause you to think, to ponder, and to pray.

"O come, let us worship and bow down: let us kneel before the Lord our maker. For he is our God; and we are the people of his pasture, and the sheep of his hand. To day if ye will hear his voice, Harden not your heart..." (Psalms 95:6-8)

The interpretations shared are the source of direct revelation to me as an individual. In the spring of 2012 I asked our Father for some specific blessings. He in turn gave me some specific "assignments". One of those was to attend the temple regularly. This resulted in me attending the temple once a week for approximately 6 months. I don't share that number to boast in any way; I share it as an example. If you wish to receive from the Father, you must be willing to DO until you BECOME what he asks of you. You cannot simply read this and expect that you are now able to receive these blessings – because you have read about them. It doesn't matter if these interpretations "make sense" or "ring true". If you are not willing to take action, they only serve as a means of condemnation as you willfully halt your progression. Mind you, I am not telling you that attending the temple is the key. The key is obedience and sacrifice. Following EVERY commandment He gives YOU. Become familiar with His voice by LISTENING and OBEYING. You don't have to be perfect, and don't expect that he requires that of you at this stage.

He wants you to be perfect, but we must progress through each law and kingdom and qualify for His blessings. We do not earn them; we qualify. Allow yourself to receive these tokens. I believe that these tokens are obtainable by all of God's children. I believe we can fulfill the law within us and progress to higher laws. I believe in personal revelation. I believe in a personal relationship with the Father, the Son and our Mother in heaven. I believe that the Book of Mormon is written as a testament of these tokens. You have the light of Christ. You are able to receive the Holy Ghost as your constant companion – as you change the robes to the other shoulder. You can then live a higher law and receive HIS spirit to always be with you. Jesus Christ will attend you; in the spirit, in the flesh, through visions, and through dreams. If we continue as a humble, faithful disciple of Christ, He will bring us to the Father. We will be admitted into His kingdom. I bear testimony of these things.

As I went to the temple I would often ask, "Where am I in the journey?" At some point in the ceremony He would answer, "Here". I would evaluate what was happening in my life at that time. Slowly the endowment and initiatory ceremony began to take the shape of a personal journey. I have received tokens, names and

signs. I only make mention of myself to provide testimony. I am not seeking for any focus to be on me. I am hoping that your energy becomes focused on Christ so that you can evolve from "I believe" to "I know"; so that you can progress from receiving a "sign" to receiving "the sure sign". Jesus Christ is the gate and few there be that find it. Don't accept the notion that your membership in any church has gained you admission into His kingdom. If you are not experiencing dreams, visions, the ministering of angels… if you have not seen Jesus the Christ, you have unbelief that must be converted to belief.

> "Or have angels ceased to appear unto the children of men? Or has he withheld the power of the Holy Ghost from them? Or will he, so long as time shall last, or the earth shall stand, or there shall be one man upon the face thereof to be saved? Behold I say unto you, Nay; for it is by faith that miracles are wrought; and it is by faith that angels appear and minister unto men; wherefore, if these things have ceased wo be unto the children of men, for it is because of unbelief, and all is vain. For no man can be saved, according to the words of Christ, save they shall have faith in his name; wherefore, if these things have ceased, then has faith ceased also; and awful is the state of man, for they are as though there had been no redemption made." (Moroni 7:36-38)

Brothers and Sisters, these principles are true. Though they may not be complete and without error, they are principles which promote Christ and the journey to be one with Him. Cause not that these things should be allowed to cease in your life. It requires effort on your part and it will happen because of your faith in the Lord Jesus Christ. In His name I share these things. Amen.

Jeremy Oakes

Jeremy Oakes

About the Author

Jeremy Oakes is a son, a brother, a grateful husband and a blessed father. He hopes to be a faithful and humble disciple of Jesus Christ - and also known as His friend.

Made in the USA
Lexington, KY
15 October 2013